This Sales Prospect Tracking Journal Belongs To:

_____

# Sales Prospecting Journal & Tracker

Every good salesman knows that you always need to be prospecting, finding new clients, and closing sales.

This prospecting journal is to be used to track your calls or contacts.

The fortune is in the follow up!


## How To Use This Journal

Record the details such as:

- Client name
- Phone number or email address
- Result (sale, booked, coming to event, etc...)
- Follow up (call again Monday, email confirmation, call in 3 months)
- And notes (needs to check schedule, was at work, call after 4pm, wants to check with wife, etc...).

You can use this notebook to schedule out all of your calls for the week ahead of time, or one day at a time.

Write in your reminders on the next page, and review them each time you get ready to call.

Maybe it's a specific product feature, or remembering to smile when you call, or maybe it's to make 5 calls per day.

Whatever it is you need to remember, write it down, so you are consistent each time you call.

Happy Selling!

# Goals

1. What are you trying to achieve with these calls/emails?

2. Set an intention for your calls.

3. What affirmations can you use to get in the right mindset for sales?

# Reminders

1. _____
2. _____
3. _____
4. _____
5. _____
6. _____
7. _____
8. _____
9. _____
10. _____
11. _____
12. _____
13. _____
14. _____
15. _____
16. _____
17. _____
18. _____
19. _____
20. _____
21. _____
22. _____
23. _____
24. _____
25. _____

| Date: | |
|---|---|
| Client Name | |
| Phone No. | |
| Result | |
| Follow Up | |
| Notes | |
| Client Name | |
| Phone No. | |
| Result | |
| Follow Up | |
| Notes | |
| Client Name | |
| Phone No. | |
| Result | |
| Follow Up | |
| Notes | |

| Date: | |
|---|---|
| Client Name | |
| Phone No. | |
| Result | |
| Follow Up | |
| Notes | |

| Client Name | |
|---|---|
| Phone No. | |
| Result | |
| Follow Up | |
| Notes | |

| Client Name | |
|---|---|
| Phone No. | |
| Result | |
| Follow Up | |
| Notes | |

| Date: | |
|---|---|
| Client Name | |
| Phone No. | |
| Result | |
| Follow Up | |
| Notes | |

| Client Name | |
|---|---|
| Phone No. | |
| Result | |
| Follow Up | |
| Notes | |

| Client Name | |
|---|---|
| Phone No. | |
| Result | |
| Follow Up | |
| Notes | |

| Date: | |
|---|---|
| Client Name | |
| Phone No. | |
| Result | |
| Follow Up | |
| Notes | |
| Client Name | |
| Phone No. | |
| Result | |
| Follow Up | |
| Notes | |
| Client Name | |
| Phone No. | |
| Result | |
| Follow Up | |
| Notes | |

| Date: | |
|---|---|
| Client Name | |
| Phone No. | |
| Result | |
| Follow Up | |
| Notes | |

| Client Name | |
|---|---|
| Phone No. | |
| Result | |
| Follow Up | |
| Notes | |

| Client Name | |
|---|---|
| Phone No. | |
| Result | |
| Follow Up | |
| Notes | |

| Date: | |
|---|---|
| Client Name | |
| Phone No. | |
| Result | |
| Follow Up | |
| Notes | |
| Client Name | |
| Phone No. | |
| Result | |
| Follow Up | |
| Notes | |
| Client Name | |
| Phone No. | |
| Result | |
| Follow Up | |
| Notes | |

| Date: | |
|---|---|
| Client Name | |
| Phone No. | |
| Result | |
| Follow Up | |
| Notes | |
| Client Name | |
| Phone No. | |
| Result | |
| Follow Up | |
| Notes | |
| Client Name | |
| Phone No. | |
| Result | |
| Follow Up | |
| Notes | |

| Date: | |
|---|---|
| Client Name | |
| Phone No. | |
| Result | |
| Follow Up | |
| Notes | |
| Client Name | |
| Phone No. | |
| Result | |
| Follow Up | |
| Notes | |
| Client Name | |
| Phone No. | |
| Result | |
| Follow Up | |
| Notes | |

| Date: | |
|---|---|
| Client Name | |
| Phone No. | |
| Result | |
| Follow Up | |
| Notes | |

| Client Name | |
|---|---|
| Phone No. | |
| Result | |
| Follow Up | |
| Notes | |

| Client Name | |
|---|---|
| Phone No. | |
| Result | |
| Follow Up | |
| Notes | |

| | |
|---|---|
| Date: | |
| Client Name | |
| Phone No. | |
| Result | |
| Follow Up | |
| Notes | |
| Client Name | |
| Phone No. | |
| Result | |
| Follow Up | |
| Notes | |
| Client Name | |
| Phone No. | |
| Result | |
| Follow Up | |
| Notes | |

| Date: | |
|---|---|
| Client Name | |
| Phone No. | |
| Result | |
| Follow Up | |
| Notes | |
| Client Name | |
| Phone No. | |
| Result | |
| Follow Up | |
| Notes | |
| Client Name | |
| Phone No. | |
| Result | |
| Follow Up | |
| Notes | |

| Date: | |
|---|---|
| Client Name | |
| Phone No. | |
| Result | |
| Follow Up | |
| Notes | |
| Client Name | |
| Phone No. | |
| Result | |
| Follow Up | |
| Notes | |
| Client Name | |
| Phone No. | |
| Result | |
| Follow Up | |
| Notes | |

| Date: | |
|---|---|
| Client Name | |
| Phone No. | |
| Result | |
| Follow Up | |
| Notes | |

| Client Name | |
|---|---|
| Phone No. | |
| Result | |
| Follow Up | |
| Notes | |

| Client Name | |
|---|---|
| Phone No. | |
| Result | |
| Follow Up | |
| Notes | |

Date:

| Client Name | |
|---|---|
| Phone No. | |
| Result | |
| Follow Up | |
| Notes | |

| Client Name | |
|---|---|
| Phone No. | |
| Result | |
| Follow Up | |
| Notes | |

| Client Name | |
|---|---|
| Phone No. | |
| Result | |
| Follow Up | |
| Notes | |

| Date: | |
|---|---|
| Client Name | |
| Phone No. | |
| Result | |
| Follow Up | |
| Notes | |

| Client Name | |
|---|---|
| Phone No. | |
| Result | |
| Follow Up | |
| Notes | |

| Client Name | |
|---|---|
| Phone No. | |
| Result | |
| Follow Up | |
| Notes | |

| Date: | |
|---|---|
| Client Name | |
| Phone No. | |
| Result | |
| Follow Up | |
| Notes | |
| Client Name | |
| Phone No. | |
| Result | |
| Follow Up | |
| Notes | |
| Client Name | |
| Phone No. | |
| Result | |
| Follow Up | |
| Notes | |

| Date: | |
|---|---|
| Client Name | |
| Phone No. | |
| Result | |
| Follow Up | |
| Notes | |

| Client Name | |
|---|---|
| Phone No. | |
| Result | |
| Follow Up | |
| Notes | |

| Client Name | |
|---|---|
| Phone No. | |
| Result | |
| Follow Up | |
| Notes | |

| Date: | |
|---|---|
| Client Name | |
| Phone No. | |
| Result | |
| Follow Up | |
| Notes | |
| Client Name | |
| Phone No. | |
| Result | |
| Follow Up | |
| Notes | |
| Client Name | |
| Phone No. | |
| Result | |
| Follow Up | |
| Notes | |

| Date: | |
|---|---|
| Client Name | |
| Phone No. | |
| Result | |
| Follow Up | |
| Notes | |
| Client Name | |
| Phone No. | |
| Result | |
| Follow Up | |
| Notes | |
| Client Name | |
| Phone No. | |
| Result | |
| Follow Up | |
| Notes | |

| Date: | |
|---|---|
| Client Name | |
| Phone No. | |
| Result | |
| Follow Up | |
| Notes | |
| Client Name | |
| Phone No. | |
| Result | |
| Follow Up | |
| Notes | |
| Client Name | |
| Phone No. | |
| Result | |
| Follow Up | |
| Notes | |

| Date: | |
|---|---|
| Client Name | |
| Phone No. | |
| Result | |
| Follow Up | |
| Notes | |

| Client Name | |
|---|---|
| Phone No. | |
| Result | |
| Follow Up | |
| Notes | |

| Client Name | |
|---|---|
| Phone No. | |
| Result | |
| Follow Up | |
| Notes | |

| Date: | |
|---|---|
| Client Name | |
| Phone No. | |
| Result | |
| Follow Up | |
| Notes | |
| Client Name | |
| Phone No. | |
| Result | |
| Follow Up | |
| Notes | |
| Client Name | |
| Phone No. | |
| Result | |
| Follow Up | |
| Notes | |

| Date: | |
|---|---|
| Client Name | |
| Phone No. | |
| Result | |
| Follow Up | |
| Notes | |

| Client Name | |
|---|---|
| Phone No. | |
| Result | |
| Follow Up | |
| Notes | |

| Client Name | |
|---|---|
| Phone No. | |
| Result | |
| Follow Up | |
| Notes | |

| Date: | |
|---|---|
| Client Name | |
| Phone No. | |
| Result | |
| Follow Up | |
| Notes | |
| Client Name | |
| Phone No. | |
| Result | |
| Follow Up | |
| Notes | |
| Client Name | |
| Phone No. | |
| Result | |
| Follow Up | |
| Notes | |

| Date: | |
|---|---|
| Client Name | |
| Phone No. | |
| Result | |
| Follow Up | |
| Notes | |
| Client Name | |
| Phone No. | |
| Result | |
| Follow Up | |
| Notes | |
| Client Name | |
| Phone No. | |
| Result | |
| Follow Up | |
| Notes | |

| Date: | |
|---|---|
| Client Name | |
| Phone No. | |
| Result | |
| Follow Up | |
| Notes | |
| Client Name | |
| Phone No. | |
| Result | |
| Follow Up | |
| Notes | |
| Client Name | |
| Phone No. | |
| Result | |
| Follow Up | |
| Notes | |

| Date: | |
|---|---|
| Client Name | |
| Phone No. | |
| Result | |
| Follow Up | |
| Notes | |

| Client Name | |
|---|---|
| Phone No. | |
| Result | |
| Follow Up | |
| Notes | |

| Client Name | |
|---|---|
| Phone No. | |
| Result | |
| Follow Up | |
| Notes | |

| Date: | |
|---|---|
| Client Name | |
| Phone No. | |
| Result | |
| Follow Up | |
| Notes | |
| Client Name | |
| Phone No. | |
| Result | |
| Follow Up | |
| Notes | |
| Client Name | |
| Phone No. | |
| Result | |
| Follow Up | |
| Notes | |

| Date: | |
|---|---|
| Client Name | |
| Phone No. | |
| Result | |
| Follow Up | |
| Notes | |

| Client Name | |
|---|---|
| Phone No. | |
| Result | |
| Follow Up | |
| Notes | |

| Client Name | |
|---|---|
| Phone No. | |
| Result | |
| Follow Up | |
| Notes | |

| Date: | |
|---|---|
| Client Name | |
| Phone No. | |
| Result | |
| Follow Up | |
| Notes | |
| Client Name | |
| Phone No. | |
| Result | |
| Follow Up | |
| Notes | |
| Client Name | |
| Phone No. | |
| Result | |
| Follow Up | |
| Notes | |

| Date: | |
|---|---|
| Client Name | |
| Phone No. | |
| Result | |
| Follow Up | |
| Notes | |

| Client Name | |
|---|---|
| Phone No. | |
| Result | |
| Follow Up | |
| Notes | |

| Client Name | |
|---|---|
| Phone No. | |
| Result | |
| Follow Up | |
| Notes | |

| Date: | |
|---|---|
| Client Name | |
| Phone No. | |
| Result | |
| Follow Up | |
| Notes | |
| Client Name | |
| Phone No. | |
| Result | |
| Follow Up | |
| Notes | |
| Client Name | |
| Phone No. | |
| Result | |
| Follow Up | |
| Notes | |

| Date: | |
|---|---|
| Client Name | |
| Phone No. | |
| Result | |
| Follow Up | |
| Notes | |
| Client Name | |
| Phone No. | |
| Result | |
| Follow Up | |
| Notes | |
| Client Name | |
| Phone No. | |
| Result | |
| Follow Up | |
| Notes | |

| Date: | |
|---|---|
| Client Name | |
| Phone No. | |
| Result | |
| Follow Up | |
| Notes | |
| Client Name | |
| Phone No. | |
| Result | |
| Follow Up | |
| Notes | |
| Client Name | |
| Phone No. | |
| Result | |
| Follow Up | |
| Notes | |

| Date: | |
|---|---|
| Client Name | |
| Phone No. | |
| Result | |
| Follow Up | |
| Notes | |

| Client Name | |
|---|---|
| Phone No. | |
| Result | |
| Follow Up | |
| Notes | |

| Client Name | |
|---|---|
| Phone No. | |
| Result | |
| Follow Up | |
| Notes | |

| Date: | |
|---|---|
| Client Name | |
| Phone No. | |
| Result | |
| Follow Up | |
| Notes | |
| Client Name | |
| Phone No. | |
| Result | |
| Follow Up | |
| Notes | |
| Client Name | |
| Phone No. | |
| Result | |
| Follow Up | |
| Notes | |

| Date: | |
|---|---|
| Client Name | |
| Phone No. | |
| Result | |
| Follow Up | |
| Notes | |
| Client Name | |
| Phone No. | |
| Result | |
| Follow Up | |
| Notes | |
| Client Name | |
| Phone No. | |
| Result | |
| Follow Up | |
| Notes | |

| Date: | |
|---|---|
| Client Name | |
| Phone No. | |
| Result | |
| Follow Up | |
| Notes | |
| Client Name | |
| Phone No. | |
| Result | |
| Follow Up | |
| Notes | |
| Client Name | |
| Phone No. | |
| Result | |
| Follow Up | |
| Notes | |

| Date: | |
|---|---|
| Client Name | |
| Phone No. | |
| Result | |
| Follow Up | |
| Notes | |
| Client Name | |
| Phone No. | |
| Result | |
| Follow Up | |
| Notes | |
| Client Name | |
| Phone No. | |
| Result | |
| Follow Up | |
| Notes | |

| Date: | |
|---|---|
| Client Name | |
| Phone No. | |
| Result | |
| Follow Up | |
| Notes | |
| Client Name | |
| Phone No. | |
| Result | |
| Follow Up | |
| Notes | |
| Client Name | |
| Phone No. | |
| Result | |
| Follow Up | |
| Notes | |

| Date: | |
|---|---|
| Client Name | |
| Phone No. | |
| Result | |
| Follow Up | |
| Notes | |
| Client Name | |
| Phone No. | |
| Result | |
| Follow Up | |
| Notes | |
| Client Name | |
| Phone No. | |
| Result | |
| Follow Up | |
| Notes | |

| Date: | |
|---|---|
| Client Name | |
| Phone No. | |
| Result | |
| Follow Up | |
| Notes | |
| Client Name | |
| Phone No. | |
| Result | |
| Follow Up | |
| Notes | |
| Client Name | |
| Phone No. | |
| Result | |
| Follow Up | |
| Notes | |

| Date: | |
|---|---|
| Client Name | |
| Phone No. | |
| Result | |
| Follow Up | |
| Notes | |
| Client Name | |
| Phone No. | |
| Result | |
| Follow Up | |
| Notes | |
| Client Name | |
| Phone No. | |
| Result | |
| Follow Up | |
| Notes | |

| Date: | |
|---|---|
| Client Name | |
| Phone No. | |
| Result | |
| Follow Up | |
| Notes | |
| Client Name | |
| Phone No. | |
| Result | |
| Follow Up | |
| Notes | |
| Client Name | |
| Phone No. | |
| Result | |
| Follow Up | |
| Notes | |

| Date: | |
|---|---|
| Client Name | |
| Phone No. | |
| Result | |
| Follow Up | |
| Notes | |
| Client Name | |
| Phone No. | |
| Result | |
| Follow Up | |
| Notes | |
| Client Name | |
| Phone No. | |
| Result | |
| Follow Up | |
| Notes | |

| Date: | |
|---|---|
| Client Name | |
| Phone No. | |
| Result | |
| Follow Up | |
| Notes | |
| Client Name | |
| Phone No. | |
| Result | |
| Follow Up | |
| Notes | |
| Client Name | |
| Phone No. | |
| Result | |
| Follow Up | |
| Notes | |

| Date: | |
|---|---|
| Client Name | |
| Phone No. | |
| Result | |
| Follow Up | |
| Notes | |

| Client Name | |
|---|---|
| Phone No. | |
| Result | |
| Follow Up | |
| Notes | |

| Client Name | |
|---|---|
| Phone No. | |
| Result | |
| Follow Up | |
| Notes | |

| Date: | |
|---|---|
| Client Name | |
| Phone No. | |
| Result | |
| Follow Up | |
| Notes | |
| Client Name | |
| Phone No. | |
| Result | |
| Follow Up | |
| Notes | |
| Client Name | |
| Phone No. | |
| Result | |
| Follow Up | |
| Notes | |

| Date: | |
|---|---|
| Client Name | |
| Phone No. | |
| Result | |
| Follow Up | |
| Notes | |
| Client Name | |
| Phone No. | |
| Result | |
| Follow Up | |
| Notes | |
| Client Name | |
| Phone No. | |
| Result | |
| Follow Up | |
| Notes | |

| Date: | |
|---|---|
| Client Name | |
| Phone No. | |
| Result | |
| Follow Up | |
| Notes | |
| Client Name | |
| Phone No. | |
| Result | |
| Follow Up | |
| Notes | |
| Client Name | |
| Phone No. | |
| Result | |
| Follow Up | |
| Notes | |

| Date: | |
|---|---|
| Client Name | |
| Phone No. | |
| Result | |
| Follow Up | |
| Notes | |
| Client Name | |
| Phone No. | |
| Result | |
| Follow Up | |
| Notes | |
| Client Name | |
| Phone No. | |
| Result | |
| Follow Up | |
| Notes | |

| Date: | |
|---|---|
| Client Name | |
| Phone No. | |
| Result | |
| Follow Up | |
| Notes | |
| Client Name | |
| Phone No. | |
| Result | |
| Follow Up | |
| Notes | |
| Client Name | |
| Phone No. | |
| Result | |
| Follow Up | |
| Notes | |

| Date: | |
|---|---|
| Client Name | |
| Phone No. | |
| Result | |
| Follow Up | |
| Notes | |
| Client Name | |
| Phone No. | |
| Result | |
| Follow Up | |
| Notes | |
| Client Name | |
| Phone No. | |
| Result | |
| Follow Up | |
| Notes | |

| Date: | |
|---|---|
| Client Name | |
| Phone No. | |
| Result | |
| Follow Up | |
| Notes | |
| Client Name | |
| Phone No. | |
| Result | |
| Follow Up | |
| Notes | |
| Client Name | |
| Phone No. | |
| Result | |
| Follow Up | |
| Notes | |

| Date: | |
|---|---|
| Client Name | |
| Phone No. | |
| Result | |
| Follow Up | |
| Notes | |
| Client Name | |
| Phone No. | |
| Result | |
| Follow Up | |
| Notes | |
| Client Name | |
| Phone No. | |
| Result | |
| Follow Up | |
| Notes | |

| Date: | |
|---|---|
| Client Name | |
| Phone No. | |
| Result | |
| Follow Up | |
| Notes | |
| Client Name | |
| Phone No. | |
| Result | |
| Follow Up | |
| Notes | |
| Client Name | |
| Phone No. | |
| Result | |
| Follow Up | |
| Notes | |

| Date: | |
|---|---|
| Client Name | |
| Phone No. | |
| Result | |
| Follow Up | |
| Notes | |
| Client Name | |
| Phone No. | |
| Result | |
| Follow Up | |
| Notes | |
| Client Name | |
| Phone No. | |
| Result | |
| Follow Up | |
| Notes | |

| Date: | |
|---|---|
| Client Name | |
| Phone No. | |
| Result | |
| Follow Up | |
| Notes | |
| Client Name | |
| Phone No. | |
| Result | |
| Follow Up | |
| Notes | |
| Client Name | |
| Phone No. | |
| Result | |
| Follow Up | |
| Notes | |

| Date: | |
|---|---|
| Client Name | |
| Phone No. | |
| Result | |
| Follow Up | |
| Notes | |

| Client Name | |
|---|---|
| Phone No. | |
| Result | |
| Follow Up | |
| Notes | |

| Client Name | |
|---|---|
| Phone No. | |
| Result | |
| Follow Up | |
| Notes | |

| Date: | |
|---|---|
| Client Name | |
| Phone No. | |
| Result | |
| Follow Up | |
| Notes | |
| Client Name | |
| Phone No. | |
| Result | |
| Follow Up | |
| Notes | |
| Client Name | |
| Phone No. | |
| Result | |
| Follow Up | |
| Notes | |

| Date: | |
|---|---|
| Client Name | |
| Phone No. | |
| Result | |
| Follow Up | |
| Notes | |
| Client Name | |
| Phone No. | |
| Result | |
| Follow Up | |
| Notes | |
| Client Name | |
| Phone No. | |
| Result | |
| Follow Up | |
| Notes | |

| Date: | |
|---|---|
| Client Name | |
| Phone No. | |
| Result | |
| Follow Up | |
| Notes | |
| Client Name | |
| Phone No. | |
| Result | |
| Follow Up | |
| Notes | |
| Client Name | |
| Phone No. | |
| Result | |
| Follow Up | |
| Notes | |

| Date: | |
|---|---|
| Client Name | |
| Phone No. | |
| Result | |
| Follow Up | |
| Notes | |
| Client Name | |
| Phone No. | |
| Result | |
| Follow Up | |
| Notes | |
| Client Name | |
| Phone No. | |
| Result | |
| Follow Up | |
| Notes | |

| Date: | |
|---|---|
| Client Name | |
| Phone No. | |
| Result | |
| Follow Up | |
| Notes | |
| Client Name | |
| Phone No. | |
| Result | |
| Follow Up | |
| Notes | |
| Client Name | |
| Phone No. | |
| Result | |
| Follow Up | |
| Notes | |

| Date: | |
|---|---|
| Client Name | |
| Phone No. | |
| Result | |
| Follow Up | |
| Notes | |
| Client Name | |
| Phone No. | |
| Result | |
| Follow Up | |
| Notes | |
| Client Name | |
| Phone No. | |
| Result | |
| Follow Up | |
| Notes | |

| Date: | |
|---|---|
| Client Name | |
| Phone No. | |
| Result | |
| Follow Up | |
| Notes | |
| Client Name | |
| Phone No. | |
| Result | |
| Follow Up | |
| Notes | |
| Client Name | |
| Phone No. | |
| Result | |
| Follow Up | |
| Notes | |

| Date: | |
|---|---|
| Client Name | |
| Phone No. | |
| Result | |
| Follow Up | |
| Notes | |
| Client Name | |
| Phone No. | |
| Result | |
| Follow Up | |
| Notes | |
| Client Name | |
| Phone No. | |
| Result | |
| Follow Up | |
| Notes | |

| Date: | |
|---|---|
| Client Name | |
| Phone No. | |
| Result | |
| Follow Up | |
| Notes | |
| Client Name | |
| Phone No. | |
| Result | |
| Follow Up | |
| Notes | |
| Client Name | |
| Phone No. | |
| Result | |
| Follow Up | |
| Notes | |

| Date: | |
|---|---|
| Client Name | |
| Phone No. | |
| Result | |
| Follow Up | |
| Notes | |
| Client Name | |
| Phone No. | |
| Result | |
| Follow Up | |
| Notes | |
| Client Name | |
| Phone No. | |
| Result | |
| Follow Up | |
| Notes | |

| Date: | |
|---|---|
| Client Name | |
| Phone No. | |
| Result | |
| Follow Up | |
| Notes | |
| Client Name | |
| Phone No. | |
| Result | |
| Follow Up | |
| Notes | |
| Client Name | |
| Phone No. | |
| Result | |
| Follow Up | |
| Notes | |

| Date: | |
|---|---|
| Client Name | |
| Phone No. | |
| Result | |
| Follow Up | |
| Notes | |
| Client Name | |
| Phone No. | |
| Result | |
| Follow Up | |
| Notes | |
| Client Name | |
| Phone No. | |
| Result | |
| Follow Up | |
| Notes | |

| Date: | |
|---|---|
| Client Name | |
| Phone No. | |
| Result | |
| Follow Up | |
| Notes | |

| Client Name | |
|---|---|
| Phone No. | |
| Result | |
| Follow Up | |
| Notes | |

| Client Name | |
|---|---|
| Phone No. | |
| Result | |
| Follow Up | |
| Notes | |

| Date: | |
|---|---|
| Client Name | |
| Phone No. | |
| Result | |
| Follow Up | |
| Notes | |
| Client Name | |
| Phone No. | |
| Result | |
| Follow Up | |
| Notes | |
| Client Name | |
| Phone No. | |
| Result | |
| Follow Up | |
| Notes | |

| Date: | |
|---|---|
| Client Name | |
| Phone No. | |
| Result | |
| Follow Up | |
| Notes | |
| Client Name | |
| Phone No. | |
| Result | |
| Follow Up | |
| Notes | |
| Client Name | |
| Phone No. | |
| Result | |
| Follow Up | |
| Notes | |

| Date: | |
|---|---|
| Client Name | |
| Phone No. | |
| Result | |
| Follow Up | |
| Notes | |
| Client Name | |
| Phone No. | |
| Result | |
| Follow Up | |
| Notes | |
| Client Name | |
| Phone No. | |
| Result | |
| Follow Up | |
| Notes | |

| Date: | |
|---|---|
| Client Name | |
| Phone No. | |
| Result | |
| Follow Up | |
| Notes | |
| Client Name | |
| Phone No. | |
| Result | |
| Follow Up | |
| Notes | |
| Client Name | |
| Phone No. | |
| Result | |
| Follow Up | |
| Notes | |

| Date: | |
|---|---|
| Client Name | |
| Phone No. | |
| Result | |
| Follow Up | |
| Notes | |
| Client Name | |
| Phone No. | |
| Result | |
| Follow Up | |
| Notes | |
| Client Name | |
| Phone No. | |
| Result | |
| Follow Up | |
| Notes | |

| Date: | |
|---|---|
| Client Name | |
| Phone No. | |
| Result | |
| Follow Up | |
| Notes | |
| Client Name | |
| Phone No. | |
| Result | |
| Follow Up | |
| Notes | |
| Client Name | |
| Phone No. | |
| Result | |
| Follow Up | |
| Notes | |

| Date: | |
|---|---|
| Client Name | |
| Phone No. | |
| Result | |
| Follow Up | |
| Notes | |
| Client Name | |
| Phone No. | |
| Result | |
| Follow Up | |
| Notes | |
| Client Name | |
| Phone No. | |
| Result | |
| Follow Up | |
| Notes | |

| Date: | |
|---|---|
| Client Name | |
| Phone No. | |
| Result | |
| Follow Up | |
| Notes | |
| Client Name | |
| Phone No. | |
| Result | |
| Follow Up | |
| Notes | |
| Client Name | |
| Phone No. | |
| Result | |
| Follow Up | |
| Notes | |

| Date: | |
|---|---|
| Client Name | |
| Phone No. | |
| Result | |
| Follow Up | |
| Notes | |
| Client Name | |
| Phone No. | |
| Result | |
| Follow Up | |
| Notes | |
| Client Name | |
| Phone No. | |
| Result | |
| Follow Up | |
| Notes | |

| Date: | |
|---|---|
| Client Name | |
| Phone No. | |
| Result | |
| Follow Up | |
| Notes | |
| Client Name | |
| Phone No. | |
| Result | |
| Follow Up | |
| Notes | |
| Client Name | |
| Phone No. | |
| Result | |
| Follow Up | |
| Notes | |

| Date: | |
|---|---|
| Client Name | |
| Phone No. | |
| Result | |
| Follow Up | |
| Notes | |
| Client Name | |
| Phone No. | |
| Result | |
| Follow Up | |
| Notes | |
| Client Name | |
| Phone No. | |
| Result | |
| Follow Up | |
| Notes | |

| Date: | |
|---|---|
| Client Name | |
| Phone No. | |
| Result | |
| Follow Up | |
| Notes | |
| Client Name | |
| Phone No. | |
| Result | |
| Follow Up | |
| Notes | |
| Client Name | |
| Phone No. | |
| Result | |
| Follow Up | |
| Notes | |

| Date: | |
|---|---|
| Client Name | |
| Phone No. | |
| Result | |
| Follow Up | |
| Notes | |

| Client Name | |
|---|---|
| Phone No. | |
| Result | |
| Follow Up | |
| Notes | |

| Client Name | |
|---|---|
| Phone No. | |
| Result | |
| Follow Up | |
| Notes | |

| Date: | |
|---|---|
| Client Name | |
| Phone No. | |
| Result | |
| Follow Up | |
| Notes | |

| Client Name | |
|---|---|
| Phone No. | |
| Result | |
| Follow Up | |
| Notes | |

| Client Name | |
|---|---|
| Phone No. | |
| Result | |
| Follow Up | |
| Notes | |

| Date: | |
|---|---|
| Client Name | |
| Phone No. | |
| Result | |
| Follow Up | |
| Notes | |
| Client Name | |
| Phone No. | |
| Result | |
| Follow Up | |
| Notes | |
| Client Name | |
| Phone No. | |
| Result | |
| Follow Up | |
| Notes | |

| Date: | |
|---|---|
| Client Name | |
| Phone No. | |
| Result | |
| Follow Up | |
| Notes | |
| Client Name | |
| Phone No. | |
| Result | |
| Follow Up | |
| Notes | |
| Client Name | |
| Phone No. | |
| Result | |
| Follow Up | |
| Notes | |

| Date: | |
|---|---|
| Client Name | |
| Phone No. | |
| Result | |
| Follow Up | |
| Notes | |
| Client Name | |
| Phone No. | |
| Result | |
| Follow Up | |
| Notes | |
| Client Name | |
| Phone No. | |
| Result | |
| Follow Up | |
| Notes | |

| Date: | |
|---|---|
| Client Name | |
| Phone No. | |
| Result | |
| Follow Up | |
| Notes | |
| Client Name | |
| Phone No. | |
| Result | |
| Follow Up | |
| Notes | |
| Client Name | |
| Phone No. | |
| Result | |
| Follow Up | |
| Notes | |

| Date: | |
|---|---|
| Client Name | |
| Phone No. | |
| Result | |
| Follow Up | |
| Notes | |
| Client Name | |
| Phone No. | |
| Result | |
| Follow Up | |
| Notes | |
| Client Name | |
| Phone No. | |
| Result | |
| Follow Up | |
| Notes | |

| Date: | |
|---|---|
| Client Name | |
| Phone No. | |
| Result | |
| Follow Up | |
| Notes | |
| Client Name | |
| Phone No. | |
| Result | |
| Follow Up | |
| Notes | |
| Client Name | |
| Phone No. | |
| Result | |
| Follow Up | |
| Notes | |

| Date: | |
|---|---|
| Client Name | |
| Phone No. | |
| Result | |
| Follow Up | |
| Notes | |
| Client Name | |
| Phone No. | |
| Result | |
| Follow Up | |
| Notes | |
| Client Name | |
| Phone No. | |
| Result | |
| Follow Up | |
| Notes | |

| Date: | |
|---|---|
| Client Name | |
| Phone No. | |
| Result | |
| Follow Up | |
| Notes | |
| Client Name | |
| Phone No. | |
| Result | |
| Follow Up | |
| Notes | |
| Client Name | |
| Phone No. | |
| Result | |
| Follow Up | |
| Notes | |

| Date: | |
|---|---|
| Client Name | |
| Phone No. | |
| Result | |
| Follow Up | |
| Notes | |

| Client Name | |
|---|---|
| Phone No. | |
| Result | |
| Follow Up | |
| Notes | |

| Client Name | |
|---|---|
| Phone No. | |
| Result | |
| Follow Up | |
| Notes | |